Put Some Pants on That Kid

a writing handbook for high school and beyond

PARENT/TEACHER GUIDE

(Student Book available separately)

Crystal Crawford

Table of Contents

What You Can Find in This Book

Week 6: Return Graded First Drafts; Discuss Revision Strategies & Techniques

Week 7: Collect Revised Drafts; Discuss Workshops (which we'll be doing the next two weeks)

Week 8: Workshop Session 1; Return graded final drafts

Week 9: Workshop Session 2

Week 10: Introducing the Argumentative Essay

Week 11: One-on-One Meetings to Review Thesis/Outline; Group-Work Activity

Week 12: Discuss Works Cited pages; Review Research Principles

Week 13: Peer Reviews; Collect First Drafts

Week 14: Return Graded First Drafts; Workshop Session 1

Week 15: Revision Week! Review Techniques/Tips for Revision

Week 16: Collect Final Drafts; In-Class Activity

Week 17: Return graded Final Drafts of Argumentative Essay; Introduce Quarter-3 Topic: Practical & Business Writing

Week 18: Introduce the Business Email/Business Letter Assignment

Week 19: Informal Peer Review of Business Letters; Collect Business Letters to Be Graded

Week 20: Return graded Business Letters; Begin Discussion of Resumes and Cover Letters

Week 21: Collect Revised Business Letters; Discuss & Collect Resumes; Review Cover Letters

Week 22: Returned Graded Resumes; Collect Cover Letters; Introduce "Chapter 14—Blogs, Online Articles, and other Public Writings"

Week 23: Collect Resubmitted Resumes; Return Graded Cover Letters; Discuss Blog Examples; Review and Collect Student-Written Blog Posts

Week 24: Return graded Resume resubmissions; Collect any revised Cover Letters; Return Graded Blog Posts; Collect Homework Questions and do a brief discussion; Workshop for Blog Posts

Week 25: Return any resubmitted Cover Letters and any other graded homework; Collect any revised Blog Posts to be re-graded; Introduce the final project for this course: the Research Paper

Week 26: Return any graded Blog Posts that were resubmitted; One-on-One Meetings to review & approve Thesis & Outline for each student; Group Activity while waiting

Week 27: Collect Annotated Bibliographies to be graded; Review Argumentative Essay concepts to prepare for writing the Research Paper

Week 28: Return graded Annotated Bibliographies; Peer Reviews; Collect First Drafts of Research Paper

Week 29: Return Graded First Drafts with Rubrics & Peer Review sheets; Allow time in class for students to work on editing/revising or to meet one-on-one with you to ask questions.

Week 30: Collect Final Drafts; Discuss Final Workshop Cycle

Week 31: Return Graded Final Drafts; Oral Presentations/ Workshop Session 1

Week 32 (the final week!): Finish Oral Presentations/Workshop Session 2; Party!

Rubrics and Essay Requirements, Checklists and Handouts

Narrative Essay Assignment

Narrative Essay Rubric

Argumentative Essay Assignment

Argumentative Essay Rubric

Research Paper Assignment

Research Paper Rubric

Other Resources

Peer Review Questions

Self-Editing Checklist

Sample Works Cited Page

Sample In-Text Citation

Acknowledgments

Contact Me

CONTACT ME

While this book comes more from my "teacher" voice as an academic writing instructor, I am also an indie author and freelance editor as well as an instructor of fiction writing. If you'd like to see more of my work, feel free to check out check out my website at **http://ccrawfordwriting.com**[1] and visit my blog with tips for writers.

I also used to work as the Director of a class program for homeschooling families called Class Source, which provides classes and support for students and home-educating families from pre-kindergarten through high school. While this textbook is my personal project and not affiliated with Class Source, my experience teaching and directing there was a major motivation for the creation of the *Put Some Pants on That Kid* materials. I have a heart for encouraging reluctant writers, and for challenging strong writers to continue to grow and improve.

You can also find me on

Facebook (**https://www.facebook.com/ccrawfordwriting/**)

Or contact me through email: **ccrawford@ccrawfordwriting.com**.

I enjoy interacting with my readers, and would love to see your comments and respond to any questions you might have!

If you're interested in hearing more about my fiction, please subscribe to my email list at **ccrawfordwriting.com/subscribe**[2] to receive updates on new releases and special happenings.

––––––––

THANK YOU FOR READING! I hope you enjoy this writing curriculum.

---

1. http://ccrawfordwriting.com/

2. http://ccrawfordwriting.com/subscribe

Put Some Pants on That Kid

a writing handbook for high school and beyond

PARENT/TEACHER GUIDE

Introduction

————

Welcome to the *Put Some Pants on That Kid* Parent/Teacher Guide, for use with the *Put Some Pants on That Kid* Student Handbook.

As a writing instructor, home-educator, and director of a class program for homeschooling families, I desire to produce materials which will be both beneficial and easy-to-use for parents and teachers, whether home-educating or teaching in an organized group setting. As such, I have provided paperback and e-book options for both the Student Book and this Parent/Teacher Guide to ensure affordability. You are welcome to purchase whichever version you prefer, as all the printable materials needed for this course are also accessible from my website. I do highly recommend that you purchase a version of the *Put Some Pants on That Kid* Student Book if you have not already, as the Student Book is the primary text, and the Lesson Plans and materials in this guide utilize readings from that Student Book as part of the core instruction. It would be best for each student to have a copy of the Student Book, or to at least have access to one, as many of the suggested assignments from this guide include readings from the text.

I explain in the introduction to the Student Book the philosophy of my *Put Some Pants on That Kid* approach to writing instruction, so I will include the brief version of it here:

> When I was studying writing in college, one of my professors emphasized the importance of proofreading and editing our work. In essence, he said, "Submitting your writing with errors and poor grammar is like sending your precious child out into the world with his shirt wrinkled and unevenly buttoned. You wouldn't want that to be the first impression people had of your child, would you? Your writing is like your child, in a way. You've worked hard on this. It matters to you. So make sure you send it out ready to give the best first impression it can."

Over the years, I have built on this analogy, and I often reference it in the writing classes I teach, but with an added twist—uneven buttons and a wrinkled shirt will give a poor first impression, but they hardly matter if the child isn't even wearing pants. The point is this: my professor was correct; grammar is important. Presentation is important. But if the larger-scale concepts aren't in place first, then you're trying to button the shirt of a kid who doesn't even have pants on, and trust me—people will *definitely* notice that. (And not in a good way.)

My hope for the Put Some Pants on That Kid Student Book is to provide straightforward, practical advice on academic and business writing for high school students and teenagers, or those preparing to enter college, where many of these types of assignments will be required. I understand that not everyone loves writing, and that's okay. I aim to make this process as straightforward and pain-free as possible, with some amusing analogies and anecdotes thrown in to the Student Book to keep things interesting.

The goal of this Parent/Teacher Guide is to provide tips for how to use the *Put Some Pants on That Kid* materials with students in an educational or classroom setting, based on how I teach these materials in my own writing classes and what I've found to be successful with my students. In this Guide, I provide suggested Lesson Plans, activities, rubrics, handouts, and more – the Lesson Plans are geared for once-per-week instructional sessions for a 32-week period, as that is the structure my classes follow. However, you could easily adapt the pacing of these lessons to fit your particular schedule. Many of the activities are also designed for group-settings. If you are working with an individual student, you could adapt the activities for solo work rather than group interaction, though I do suggest finding some other students to collaborate with if possible, particularly for Peer Reviews and Workshop sessions, as these sessions provide valuable external feedback for the growing writer.

All the handouts and checklists provided in this guide (and in the *Put Some Pants on That Kid* Student Book) are also available in printable format on my website. The link is provided later in this guide. These printable materials are free to print, copy, and use – both for your personal use and for your students, though I do ask that you not attempt to sell or otherwise financially profit from those materials, as they are a free resource provided as an accompaniment to this book. More information about usage of these resources is available at the link provided.

If you have any questions about how to use *Put Some Pants on That Kid* with your students, or would like clarification on anything included in this guide, please feel free to email me at **ccrawford@ccrawfordwriting.com**. I would be happy to answer your questions, as my hope is for this guide and the accompanying textbook to be beneficial for both you and your students.

Sincerely,

Crystal Crawford

Author, Editor, and Writing Instructor

http://ccrawfordwriting.com[1]

ccrawford@ccrawfordwriting.com

http://facebook.com/ccrawfordwriting

---

1. **http://ccrawfordwriting.com/**

How to Use This Parent/Teacher Guide

You are certainly free to use this guide in whichever way most benefits you. However, here are my suggestions for making the most of these materials:

1. I highly recommend you purchase a copy of the *Put Some Pants on That Kid* Student Book, even if you do not plan to have your student(s) read it directly. The primary content and writing instruction is all contained in the Student Book; this Parent/Teacher Guide is simply intended as a supplement to facilitate your use of the Student Book in instructing your students and guiding them through the writing process. The Lesson Plans included in this guide reference suggested readings for students from the Student Book, as well as recommended content from within those readings for you to review as the instructor prior to each lesson. The Student Book is available in both paperback and in e-book to ensure affordability, and all of the printables are included free of cost (more on that later). While you could attempt to use only the content here in the Parent/Teacher Guide and the printables without the Student Book, the system works far better when all pieces are used in conjunction.

2. If you are teaching in a group setting, start by reviewing the Using the Lesson Plans in a Classroom Setting section which immediately follows this one. It provides an overview of my recommended approaches to writing instruction, including tips on giving feedback on student projects and grading assignments. The Tips for Providing Feedback on Students' Papers is perhaps *the most* important section of this entire guide. Even if you read nothing else in this book, please read that, as your feedback will set the tone for the students' entire writing experience. The Detailed Lesson Plans, Weekly Schedule, and more are included following that section.

3. If you are working with an individual student rather than teaching in a group setting, feel free to skim over the sections of this guide which

are not applicable to you. You will probably find the most value in the Tips for Providing Feedback, Weekly Schedule, Detailed Lesson Plans, and Rubrics and Essay Requirements sections.

4. I just have to say this once more, for emphasis: Please read the Tips for Providing Feedback on Students' Papers section. It is the heart of the entire *Put Some Pants on That Kid* approach to writing instruction.

5. As mentioned in the introduction, additional copies of all Rubrics, handouts, etc. provided in this book can be printed from my website. You can find them here: **https://www.ccrawfordwriting.com/pspotk-printables**

Using the Lesson Plans in a Classroom Setting

———

Because the Lesson Schedule dives straight in to the individual lessons, first I wanted to provide some additional information about using *Put Some Pants on That Kid* as a text for classroom or group instruction.

Again, this is all based on *my* preferences for how to implement this material. You may need to adapt some of it for your particular circumstances or goals, but I hope this section at least provides a helpful foundation.

An Overall Note on Grading Assignments

FOR MY WRITING CLASS based on this material, I use the following grading system:

Grading:

- Outlines/Planning—10%
- First Drafts—20%
- Revisions/Editing—20%
- Final Drafts—20% (you will notice these are not weighted more than earlier drafts; this is because *every* step of this process matters!)
- Workshops—10%
- Weekly Online Topic Discussions—10%
- Class Participation — 10%

0-59 = F; 60-69=D; 70-79=C; 80-89=B; 90-100=A

I use a weighted online gradebook (I believe you can even find some for free!) and then created weighted categories for each of the above. Then, when I input assignments, I just choose which category that assignment belongs in, and the program automatically calculates the proper weighting into the student's overall grade in the class.

You can absolutely grade using a different system. In fact, if you're doing this in a small or individual setting, some of the categories I've listed may not apply. However, I wanted to provide a glimpse at my personal system just for clarity.

I do one workshop per quarter, and I provide a weekly online discussion prompt to accompany students' homework assignments. I use a closed Facebook group for class discussions, but you could use another forum or just omit the online discussion if you prefer. I like the sense of community and ongoing dialogue the online discussions provide, particularly since my classes meet only once per week. I provide more details about each of these in the following pages.

You could also do all these assignments *ungraded* and simply provide feedback for improvement; however, in class settings I find that assigning grades is a standard, easily understood way to measure a student's progress through the materials.

Tips for Providing Feedback on Students' Papers (PLEASE READ!)

I PROBABLY SHOULD HAVE put this section in huge font somewhere at the beginning of this book, just to make sure everyone saw it... but I didn't want to be pushy, so I settled for just adding PLEASE READ to this section on the Table of Contents.

In my opinion, the lifeblood—the absolute *most* important part—of teaching essay writing (whether in a classroom or one-on-one tutoring) is *the feedback you write in the margins of your student's paper.*

I first learned to write quality marginal comments when I was a TA in grad school, and then I began to apply that to my freelance editing projects... it is 100% the reason my clients request me again and again as an editor, and also the best way I've found to not only *correct* a student's writing, but to *teach* the student how to improve their own writing in future drafts.

Most of my papers in school were collected only once and graded, with little feedback other than a percentage written in pen at the top. At the time, it was just normal… but now that as an instructor I've experienced the magic of collecting multiple drafts, providing detailed feedback, and having students rewrite, I'll never go back! It does take a *lot* more time, but the leaps and bounds students make as a result are more than worth it.

I am not an educational expert by any means (my degree is in writing, not education), but I have been doing this writing-instructor-and-editor thing for a while with good results, so I want to provide some tips here for those of you who may be newer to this. Feedback in the margins *does* require that you have a basic grasp of writing skills, but if you've read this textbook, you should have enough information to provide basic feedback on different elements of the student's writing.

Techniques for Providing Valuable Feedback in the Margins of a Student's Paper:

Compliment Sandwich!

I know, it's like a sit-com phrase, but seriously… it's important. No matter how many corrections I find a paper needs, after reading the whole essay, I do two things: (1) I write a little note at the end praising them for something they did well (even if it's just "Great job completing this draft on time!"), and (2) I write a small paragraph at the *top* of the paper with a summary of my overall feedback, and intentionally work in praise (pointing out one or two things I feel the essay did well) so that the student will see that positive feedback *first* before getting into any of the specific critiques or corrections. Often this summary paragraph at the top of the paper will say something like "There are some corrections needed, but," followed with what the student did well, and then end with another positive like "I look forward to seeing how strong this essay becomes in your next draft!" Starting and ending on a positive note really does make the corrective feedback easier to take, and prevents discouraging any students who may already be struggling or feeling overwhelmed.

Find What's *Right*, Not Just What's Wrong.

This is similar to the previous point, but more about what you write in the margins *in between* your sandwiched praise. Too often, students grow discouraged because a paper comes back with red marks all over it, and every mark denotes something they did "wrong." I've heard some teachers say they don't grade in red because it's too aggressive. (I do sometimes use red, but I prefer purple or another fun color instead; glitter pens are great, too!) However, this is less about the color and more about the content. Yes, you can mark errors throughout the essay; these corrections give the student a focus for editing and instruction for how to proceed on their next draft. But the student also needs positive reinforcement—little statements of what they did well, or even comments from you saying, "Oh wow, this is an interesting idea; I wouldn't have thought of that!" or "This was worded clearly and concisely; good job!" These statements have far more impact than you might imagine, and go a long way toward encouraging writers, especially the student who sees him- or herself as "just not good a writer." (Also feel free to add smiley-faces or illustrative doodles in the margins; I sometimes do. Sure, it may feel "unprofessional," but it makes the process a lot more fun for both you and the student and usually brings a smile which can help the negative feedback get digested a bit more easily. You don't *have* to doodle on their papers, of course, but the point is that you *can*.)

Go Deep

To borrow the phrase my faculty advisor used with me—*Go Deeper* with your feedback. It's so easy to focus on the glaring, surface-level issues like misspellings, punctuation, and poor grammar. But those things are only scratching the surface. Even if the student fixed *all* of those types of errors, if the underlying content and organization wasn't solid, the essay would still flop. When I'm providing feedback, I mark errors that jump out at me as I'm reading, but I'm focusing on other things instead—is there a clear thesis? Is the essay structured in a way that makes sense? Does it build progressively toward an impact? Are the elements of a strong introduction and conclusion in place? Are the body paragraphs logically organized? I provide marginal comments on these types of issues, sometimes writing—no exaggeration—full paragraphs on each comment explaining not only where the student perhaps went off-course, but basic suggestions on how to fix it. If you're unsure how to tackle these types of issues within an essay, use the Rubrics I provide in this book as a starting point... they provide some clear, objective measures against which you can compare a student's essay to see if the essay has any deeper-level issues which need to be addressed. Once those are handled, *then* you can focus on grammar and punctuation. I tend to do only a cursory search for Grammar & Mechanics in the first draft, focusing on the larger-scale issues instead, and then crack down on the grammar in subsequent drafts, once the bigger issues should have already been addressed. The point structure I use in the Grammar section of the Rubrics is ideal for this, since it doesn't take off for individual errors, but rather awards points for the *absence* of certain types of Grammar & Punctuation errors. This means if I don't catch every error in their first drafts, their grades won't plummet on the next draft when I pay more attention to that aspect. I also inform students that this is my system, so they don't balk if I didn't catch a particular error in the first draft but find it in a later one.

Be Specific

Statements like "This essay is confusing," or "This doesn't make a clear argument" are often too generic for the student to comprehend and implement during editing. When you hit an aspect of the essay that doesn't seem up to par, take a moment to consider *why*. What, specifically, about the essay left me confused? Perhaps it lacked transitions to connect one paragraph to the next, or didn't provide enough supporting evidence to explain one of its arguments, or presented the topics in an order that didn't progress logically. *These* types of comments—written in the margin next to the exact places where the essay derailed—are far more helpful than a generic, all-encompassing statement.

Suggest, Don't Solve

I had an instructor in grad school who would return papers with every error not only marked but *corrected*, and then allow us to resubmit for a higher grade. Wow, did that make the editing and revision process a snap! The problem was, it also didn't make me fully engage my brain—I'd just copy over whatever she'd written into my new version, and send it in knowing she'd approve; they were her ideas! I discourage this level of correction for high school level writers (and beyond). They learn far more if they're shown what's wrong and given some direction, yet expected to figure out and implement the corrections on their own. When I find simple errors like comma faults, rather than marking the correct placement of the comma I circle it and write "comma issue—please fix." If I find a problem with the thesis, rather than rewriting it, I'll write a note that says, "The thesis doesn't have three distinct prongs; please rewrite it before moving forward." (This is another reason I collect the Thesis and Outline for review before the students ever begin drafting; deep-level issues like a poorly written thesis can mean the entire paper needs to be rewritten! It's best to catch those beforehand.) If a student is struggling with a particular issue, then I may provide an example of how they *could* fix it, something like "This sentence needs to be rewritten so that it more clearly presents the argument. Try a more definite statement like... [insert example here]... but in your own words." There's a careful balance between providing students the feedback they need to improve, and doing the work *for* them. Let's face it: writing is hard at first, it's a process, and there's no shortcut to getting better than to just *do it*, again and again and again. Students may not love this, but once they see the progress in their subsequent drafts and begin to feel more confident about implementing feedback, they usually complain a little less. Please, please, *please* resist the urge to just edit and correct everything for the student. They need to go through the learning process of doing it themselves.

How to Utilize "Workshops" in the Classroom

AS I MENTIONED, I DO one workshop per quarter for a 32-week course (roughly one round of workshops every 8 weeks of classes). This is because I structured the class so that each quarter we're covering a different Section of this book. The workshops are a chance to deepen the understanding of what was covered in that quarter's Section, and to build a sense of community and support between the writers in the classroom. I teach a lot of writing classes heavy on collaboration (and have taken several myself), and I've found that writing cooperatively creates an amazing connection and bond between students, providing a network of encouragement and support they can tap into—sometimes for years to come. Because essays are usually written independently, the Workshops are a way to implement this sense of collaboration in the classroom by getting students involved and invested in each other's writing.

In the text of this book, I sometimes refer to a more generic version of this as a Peer Review; however, in my lesson plans we'll be doing both basic Peer Reviews (once per assignment) and special group sessions which take the Peer Review concept a bit farther (once per quarter). You'll see these special sessions referred to as Workshops. Details on how and when I use these during the 32-week course are provided in the appropriate weeks of the Lesson Schedule.

Each quarter's essay assignments will move through several drafts (outline, first draft, and at least one revision). At least one draft of each assignment will be *workshopped*, meaning classmates will read each other's writing and offer feedback/critiques. This is done in a positive, encouraging environment and I intentionally set expectations ahead of time for how to both give and receive critiques. The Peer Review/Workshop is such an important part of the learning process and provides an excellent opportunity for students to learn and grow by identifying writing done well and adapting examples into their own writing, learning from one another's strengths.

How to Use Weekly Online Discussions

AS I MENTIONED BEFORE, I provide a weekly online discussion prompt to accompany students' homework assignments, and I generally use a private Facebook group as the location for these discussions. Some parents are not comfortable with their kids having personal Facebook accounts. That's okay! I suggest that the parent join the private group with *his or her own* account and then allow the student to check the notifications and discussion regularly. In the several years I've been doing this, I've never had a family completely refuse to use Facebook once I've provided these options. However, if you—or some of your students' families—are uncomfortable with using Facebook for class discussions, there are plenty of other free options, including Google Classroom, other online class platforms, and a variety of free websites/online forum hosts which would allow you to set up a private location with password access. When I taught ENC 1101, the students used a password-protected Wiki to collaboratively write projects, but I imagine that something similar could be used for discussions. In a pinch, you could always go with Google Docs. It allows you to create a private document (accessible only by email addresses which are given access) and has editing, comment, and chat features. A Google Doc for that week's discussion prompt with the Comments feature opened would suffice for online discussions.

Sometimes the weekly prompts for these online discussions relate directly to the topic of that week's class, and sometimes they are just about writing in general. The online discussions are not an essential part of the class, but they add a wonderful layer of community and engagement. If you meet only once or twice per week for class, as we do, then I recommend implementing these online discussions as a way of reinforcing concepts and keeping dialogue open throughout the week. I also allow students to post questions about the assignments/content in the discussion forums, and then I answer them there in the forum... that way any other students who may have had the same question can also see the answer, or other students can chime in if they know the answers and I haven't yet responded. I also occasionally post silly memes or other writing-related things in the discussion group—I like to make the class experience as fun and engaging as possible, and the online discussion group has been a wonderful way of making that happen both in and out of the classroom.

32-Week Lesson Schedule

―――

To home educators and other instructors:

This schedule is recommended for a classroom setting of 9th-11th grade students. It can work for classes and groups of varying sizes; it is best suited for a class large enough to break into small groups, but could be adapted for smaller classes as well. I explain below each week how I implement that lesson through instruction, group-work, etc., in the classroom. I also include recommended readings from *Put Some Pants on That Kid* to accompany each week. The instructions listed on the Lesson Schedule are suggestions. You can adapt as needed for more advanced students or independent studies. Please also feel free to adjust this suggested schedule to your students' needs—spend more time on a topic if needed to ensure retention/mastery before moving forward, and omit topics which do not apply to your class or situation.

The classes I teach meet one day per week, so the lesson plans and assignments listed below are geared that way: there is one concentrated lesson per week (just over an hour of instruction time), and then I provide at-home assignments for the students to do throughout the rest of the week. You can adapt this to your own needs, expanding the lessons into shorter periods over several days if need be, and breaking up the homework however you see fit during the week. The at-home assignments grow in complexity as the course progresses; the first few weeks are relatively simple to ease students into the course.

To those using this as a self-guided study:

Please adjust this suggested schedule to accommodate your specific needs. If certain topics do not apply to you, then simply review those chapters and move on if desired, devoting more time to the topics most useful to your current needs and desired growth areas.

Weekly Schedule of Topics

WEEK 1: Welcome and Introduction to Class; In-class Writing Assignment

Week 2: Basic Essay Structure; Simple Introduction to the Narrative Essay

Week 3: Introducing the First Essay Assignment!

Week 4: One-on-One Meetings to Review Students' Theses & Outlines; Group-Work for Students while Waiting

Week 5: Collecting the First Draft; Peer Reviews; a Brief Discussion of Citing Sources

Week 6: Return Graded First Drafts; Discuss Revision Strategies & Techniques

Week 7: Collect Revised Drafts; Discuss Workshops (which we'll be doing the next two weeks)

Week 8: Workshop Session 1; Return graded final drafts

Week 9: Workshop Session 2

Week 10: Introducing the Argumentative Essay

Week 11: One-on-One Meetings to Review Thesis/Outline; Group-Work Activity

Week 12: Discuss Works Cited pages; Review Research Principles

Week 13: Peer Reviews; Collect First Drafts

Week 14: Return Graded First Drafts; Workshop Session 1

Week 15: Revision Week! Review Techniques/Tips for Revision

Week 16: Collect Final Drafts; In-Class Activity

Week 17: Return graded Final Drafts of Argumentative Essay; Introduce Quarter-3 Topic: Practical & Business Writing

Week 18: Introduce the Business Email/Business Letter Assignment

Week 19: Informal Peer Review of Business Letters; Collect Business Letters to Be Graded

Week 20: Return graded Business Letters; Begin Discussion of Resumes and Cover Letters

Week 21: Collect Revised Business Letters; Discuss & Collect Resumes; Review Cover Letters

Week 22: Returned Graded Resumes; Collect Cover Letters; Introduce "Chapter 14—Blogs, Online Articles, and other Public Writings"

Week 23: Collect Resubmitted Resumes; Return Graded Cover Letters; Discuss Blog Examples; Review and Collect Student-Written Blog Posts

Week 24: Return graded Resume resubmissions; Collect any revised Cover Letters; Return Graded Blog Posts; Collect Homework Questions and do a brief discussion; Workshop for Blog Posts

Week 25: Return any resubmitted Cover Letters and any other graded homework; Collect any revised Blog Posts to be re-graded; Introduce the final project for this course: the Research Paper

Week 26: Return any graded Blog Posts that were resubmitted; One-on-One Meetings to review & approve Thesis & Outline for each student; Group Activity while waiting

Week 27: Collect Annotated Bibliographies to be graded; Review Argumentative Essay concepts to prepare for writing the Research Paper

Week 28: Return graded Annotated Bibliographies; Peer Reviews; Collect First Drafts of Research Paper

Week 29: Return Graded First Drafts with Rubrics & Peer Review sheets; Allow time in class for students to work on editing/revising or to meet one-on-one with you to ask questions.

Week 30: Collect Final Drafts; Discuss Final Workshop Cycle

Week 31: Return Graded Final Drafts; Oral Presentations/Workshop Session 1

Week 32 (the final week!): Finish Oral Presentations/Workshop Session 2; Party!

Detailed Lesson Plans

Week 1: Welcome and Introduction to Class; In-Class Writing Assignment

I GO OVER THE SCOPE of the class and what we'll be covering, and open a group discussion with students on their experiences in past writing classes: were those experiences positive or negative? Why? I emphasize that all answers are safe; they do not *have* to enjoy writing. In fact, one of the main goals of such a class is to help reluctant writers find techniques that will make writing less daunting.

I then give an in-class writing assignment which I used to assess current student writing levels (this will be graded only as a complete/incomplete, not given a letter grade). This is a loose Narrative Essay with few requirements. I give students limited directions for this first assignment, simply asking them to write in first-person (I/my), and to write at least 1 page. I use the prompt: *How do you feel about writing (like/dislike; confident/anxious; etc.) and why?* Allow 25-30 minutes in class for this writing; minimum of 1 page handwritten. (This in-class writing will be used to identify the key strengths and areas of improvement for the students in the class; this will determine which specific topics you may need to spend extra time with in the following weeks.) I collect them in class but read them at home, noting any specific writing aspects the students seem to struggle with so I can add them to class discussions as we go.

Homework for Week 1: Read "Introduction" from *Put Some Pants on That Kid*. Based on this reading and this week's class discussion, answer the following on a sheet of paper:

1. Why is it important to develop strong writing skills?
2. Do you feel you have strong writing skills? Why or why not?
3. How do you think strong writing skills will benefit you in your future plans? (This may include educational goals, career goals, hobbies, etc.)

*Note on grading this week's homework: These are personal questions with no definite right/wrong answers. I usually write some encouraging comments in the margin and then grade them according to completion (if all three questions were answered, it's 100%, if only two questions were answered, then roughly 66%, and so on). Clarify that the grading—if not 100%—was due to the assignment being incomplete, not to the student's answers being "wrong."

Online Discussion Post for Week 1: Create an introductory prompt to ease students in to interacting in the online discussion. I do something like, "Welcome to the Discussion Group! Comment below with what you like to do in your free time, so we know you're here!" (You could basically use anything—favorite pet, favorite book, etc.—the purpose is to break the ice.)

Week 2: Basic Essay Structure; Simple Introduction to the Narrative Essay

THIS WEEK IS ALL ABOUT the basics. I talk about basic essay structure and how there are different types of essays, each with its own set of requirements and expectations. I discuss basic 5-prong structure (intro, conclusion, and 3 body paragraphs in between), and the concepts of thesis and hook. I then jump straight into the first type of essay we'll be covering in this class: the Narrative Essay. I use the in-class writing assignment from the previous week as a starting point, explaining that what they wrote was a reflective narrative, though a loose one. Now we'll be learning the expectations for structured Narrative Essays. We talk about the elements expected from a Narrative Essay, as well as more general concepts like voice, rhetorical devices, and knowing your audience. (If you're unfamiliar with any of these concepts, you can read "Chapter 1—The Basics" ahead of time; it explains all this in detail. Students will read that chapter for homework to review what was covered in class, and then answer some questions to help them internalize the information they've heard and read this week.)

I do lots of notes on the board during the class discussion, making lists and charts to differentiate visually between generic essay requirements and those of Narrative Essays. Some students are visual learners, so this aspect is important for retention of information. I also try to involve the students as much as possible, using the Socratic Method (asking questions for them to answer rather than delivering the information strictly as a lecture). For example, I might begin the discussion with "How many of you have written a 5-paragraph essay before? Okay, great. Can you tell me what each of the five paragraphs usually includes?" Then I make notes on the board, writing down their answers... if some of them give almost-correct answers, I give a nudge, something like "You've got the right idea, but there's an official term for that. Does anyone know the terminology?" If someone gives a wildly incorrect answer, I try not to shoot it down. Instead, I attempt to redirect with something like, "That's not quite what I was looking for, but I like that we've got ideas flowing now! Does anyone else have a guess?" **I am including these tips here because it is _so important_ to me that I make writing a positive experience for my students...** many of them come in already dreading writing or only taking the class because someone has forced them. I know it's unrealistic to make all my students love writing, but that doesn't mean I can't create an encouraging, up-building classroom environment that bolsters their confidences and creates positively associated experiences with writing. This is also the reason I provide plenty of comments in the margins of students' writing assignments, making sure to point out what they've done well, not only what needs improvement.

Homework for Week 2: Read "Chapter 1—The Basics" from *Put Some Pants on That Kid*. Then answer the following questions on a sheet of paper:

1. What is the primary goal of a *narrative*?
2. What are the three main things a typical essay "should" do?
3. What are the five additional things a *Narrative Essay* should include?
4. What is *authorial voice*?
5. In your own words, define *point of view*.
6. What are the three rhetorical devices mentioned, and what does each mean?
7. Why is it important to know your audience?

*Note on grading this week's homework: all the answers are stated in "Chapter 1—The Basics." You should be able to use that chapter as an answer key for this assignment. Unless the question asked for exact terminology, I mark an answer correct if it shows understanding of the concept, even if the student used different wording.

Online Discussion Post for Week 2: This week we're learning about *ethos, pathos,* and *logos*. Find a company which utilizes one of these three rhetorical devices in their marketing ads, either online, on television, in a magazine, on a billboard, etc. In the comments below, describe the ad you've chosen and specify which device(s) the ad uses and how the ad demonstrates the device(s).

Week 3: Introducing the First Essay Assignment!

THIS WEEK I PROVIDE students with the Narrative Essay Requirements sheet and the Narrative Essay Rubric, and go over both in class. (You can find both documents in the Appendix of *Put Some Pants on That Kid* or in the Rubrics and Essay Requirements section of this handbook.) I open up discussion for questions about the requirements for the Narrative Essay, then move into a discussion of the different steps/multiple drafts I'll be collecting for this assignment. The first step on the list is an Outline and Thesis, so I spend some time writing examples on the board (or you can print out examples ahead of time to hand out—I provide some in "Chapter 2—Planning and Outlining Your Narrative Essay"). Allow time for questions or clarifications, since the Outline and Thesis will be part of the homework for this week.

Homework for Week 3: Read "Chapter 2—Planning and Outlining Your Narrative Essay." Create a Thesis and an Outline for your Narrative Essay, and type them out. Bring your typed Thesis & Outline to the next class; you'll be meeting one-on-one with me to review them.

Online Discussion Post for Week 3: What type(s) of brainstorming/planning techniques did you employ this week while working on your Thesis & Outline? Did any of them work better for you than others? Comment below!

Week 4: One-on-One Meetings to Review Students' Theses & Outlines; Group-Work for Students while Waiting

IN CLASS THIS WEEK, I meet with students one-on-one to review and discuss each student's Thesis and Outline. I'm looking for a few things in this review: (1) that it meets the assignment requirements, (2) that the thesis is strong and specific enough to support a full Narrative Essay, and (3) that the outline stays focused around that thesis, while also providing enough supporting details to fully expand the narrative. I also do a quick check that a hook concept seems to be in place for the intro, and that the student's proposed narrative is organized in a way that makes sense. If anything is off, I take time to discuss with the student and help them tweak the Thesis & Outline right then and there, so they're leaving class with everything they need for drafting this week. These individual meetings take time, so depending on class size, it may be all you're able to do in this week's class—you may even need to arrange extra time after class to give additional aid to students whose theses/outlines still need work. The priority is ensuring each student has a solid Thesis & Outline, since this week's homework will be to use those plans to write the first draft of the essay.

While you're meeting with a student, the rest of the class needs something to do. Before I call students over to meet with me one-on-one, I split the class into small groups and write a group activity on the board for them to do while I'm in meetings. Then, each student just slips out of the group as I call his/her name, and returns to the group when the meeting is done. I like to use an activity which relates to the essay we're about to write, so for this week, a great one is a Sensory Detail activity as practice for using sensory details in their writing. I have the students examine the classroom, and in groups, make a joint list of all sensory details they could use to describe the classroom. Each group should come up with *at least* five sensory details about the classroom for each sense (touch, taste, smell, hearing, sight, sound). The challenge is to be creative, and try to think of ways to describe these sensory details which also involve imagery (for example, "the carpet is as brown as a toad"). If there's time after I've met with all students, I have the groups share their lists of sensory details with the class.

Homework for Week 4: Read "Chapter 3—Tips for Writing Your Narrative Essay," then (you guessed it) *write the first draft of your Narrative Essay*. Use the tips included in the chapter to help you, as well as the Requirements & Rubric sheets for this assignment. Type up your first draft, print it, and bring it to the next class!

*Note to instructors: Be sure to emphasize the need for students to allow plenty of time for this week's homework! Drafting may take more time than they expect.

Online Discussion Post for Week 4: Were there any tips in this week's chapter you hadn't thought of before, or which you found particularly helpful? Comment below.

Week 5: Collecting the First Draft; Peer Reviews; a Brief Discussion of Citing Sources

I START THIS WEEK'S class by asking students to hold on to their first draft essays (there's always at least one eager to get rid of it and turn it in the moment class starts!), explaining that we'll be using them in class for something in a few minutes. With that established, I then transition into an overview of the need for citing sources. I discuss and define plagiarism, and explain that though this essay assignment did not *require* the use of outside sources, if they used any (quotations to set the mood, anecdotes or references from people other than the writer him/herself, etc.), that they must be sure to properly cite those sources. Chapter 4 (which they'll be reading for homework this week) will explain more about how to do that for this assignment if they need to, but it's a topic much class time will be spent on later in the course, when we move into Argumentative Essays and Research Papers.

I then divide them into pairs (a group of three works, too, if you have an odd number of students), and give each student a copy of the Peer Review Questions sheet (available in this book). Students swap essays (yes, they actually have to give their first drafts to each other to read!), and then read each other's essays while using the Peer Review sheet to provide feedback. When they're done, each student should give the essay and Peer Review sheet (with their feedback) back to the original writer of the essay. The writer can read the Peer Review and ask questions and make notes for themselves as needed.

When students are all done with the Peer Reviews, I collect both the first draft essays (which may now have peer comments on them) *and* the Peer Review sheets. I'll be grading both—the Peer Reviewer gets credit for the review, and I add additional notes and feedback to both the Peer Review sheet (if I agree/ disagree with the peer's feedback, I may note this for the essay writer) and to the First Draft essay (using marginal comments as I explain in the section of the Parent/Teacher Guide on writing feedback on essays). I then grade the student's essay draft using a copy of the Rubric for the Narrative Essay and attach the Rubric to the essay. At next week's class, I'll be returning the Essay/Rubric *and* the Peer Review to each student—not to the reviewer, but to the student whose essay was reviewed—so that the student has a plethora of feedback to use in revising their essay that week.

Homework for Week 5: Read "Chapter 4—Citing Sources & Avoiding Plagiarism: Crafting a Works Cited Page" and create a Works Cited page for your essay if you need it. (If not, just read the chapter; these are important concepts we'll be building on later in this course.)

Online Discussion for Week 5: What did you learn from "Chapter 4—Citing Sources & Avoiding Plagiarism" that you didn't know before reading? If you already knew everything in this chapter, then comment what you think is the most important element covered in Chapter 4.

*Note to instructors: This week's discussion post also serves as a way for you to verify that students are doing the weekly reading. If you suspect a student isn't, now's a good time to contact that student and emphasize the importance of reading these foundational chapters (they're only a few pages each!) so they don't fall behind later in the course when we refer back to some of these concepts.

Week 6: Return Graded First Drafts; Discuss Revision Strategies & Techniques

IF YOU'RE UNFAMILIAR with revision strategies, read "Chapter 5—The Revising & Editing Process" before teaching this week's class.

Students are always eager to see their graded drafts (or perhaps anxious), but I've found that returning the drafts too soon can be a major distraction. So I like to hold the drafts until after we do a basic discussion, then return them with enough time left for students to ask questions about my feedback on their papers, if they desire.

I explain the above to the students, and then begin a discussion of Revision & Editing—the different levels of editing, various techniques for editing & revision, etc. I go through the content of Chapter 5 there in class and clarify any confusion, so that when students read the chapter for homework this week, it will be review and not entirely new.

After this discussion, I hand back the graded essays & Peer Reviews, and give students a couple minutes to look through them. I then open the floor to questions that students feel comfortable asking, especially if the whole class may benefit from hearing the answer—such as "What do you mean by a comma fault" or "Can you give an example of a hook?" I answer any of these, writing examples on the board. I then tell students they can talk softly for the last few minutes of class, while I make myself available over to the side for any students who have questions they'd rather discuss with me privately.

Homework for Week 6: Read "Chapter 5—The Revising & Editing Process," then edit & rewrite your essay into a new draft, using the tips from that chapter and the feedback from your Peer Review, graded Rubric, and instructor comments on your first draft. Type up your new draft, print it, and bring it to next class. This draft will be re-graded using the Rubric for your final grade on this project.

Online Discussion Post for Week 6: (1) Did you have difficulty revising and editing your paper? Why or why not? (2) Did you find any tips from Chapter

5 helpful for revising your essay? Which tips? Comment your answers to these two questions below.

Week 7: Collect Revised Drafts; Discuss Workshops (which we'll be doing the next two weeks)

THIS WEEK, I COLLECT the revised drafts at the beginning of class, and set them aside. I'll be grading them over the week, using a clean copy of the same Narrative Essay Rubric I used for the first draft, and the graded papers will be returned to students the following week.

The important content for this week's class is to outline the structure for the Workshops we'll be doing in class for the last 2 weeks of this quarter, and to ensure all students come prepared the following week. Although students have already submitted their final drafts for this essay, there is still a lot to be learned from Workshopping their writing which can then be implemented on future projects (plus, this ensures that the version the classmates see is the student's best effort).

The Workshop will function as follows:

- Each student will bring a *clean* printed copy of his or her final draft of the essay (*clean* meaning it doesn't have any notes or grades on it; it is just the printed final draft—the copy they gave me will be kept separate, as it will have grades and feedback on it)
- At the start of class, we will put all the essays in a stack. Each student will then come and take a copy of one essay (not his or her own) and sit down to read it. The student will not make notes or feedback, simply read. When finished, the student will return the copy to the table and grab a new one from the stack. I will allot 30 minutes of class for reading essays this way; however many the students can get through in that time.
- When the reading time is up, all essays go back to the table, and we form up into a circle for discussion. I will grab an essay from the table and read the title or summarize what it's about and then ask how many students read that essay. I will make a list on the board of how many read each essay, then we start discussion on the essay with the most readers, discuss it, and then move to the next essay on the list

(this way, we're giving our best chance at a quality group discussion since hopefully a decent number of the students read that essay).

- The discussion itself is simple—I write two questions on the board: "What did the writer do *well*?" and "What could the writer improve?" We start with the "did well" list, then give a minute or two for quick notes on improvement at the end.
- The student who wrote the essay is not permitted to interject or explain during the discussion, only to take notes if desired. However, he or she may ask questions for clarification after the discussion of his/her essay has completed.
- Get through as many essays as you reasonably can in this way, and the rest will be saved for next week, when we'll repeat the process again.

*Note: This workshop format can be *very* intimidating for some students if they aren't used to having their writing read by others. However, it is *so valuable* for the learning and growth process, as it helps students learn to be open to critique and feedback, but does so in a controlled, encouraging environment. Because of this, be sure to emphasize to students beforehand that any comments or feedback made should be considerate and respectful, that we are looking to highlight what each writer did *well* so we can learn from one another, and that any critiques or suggestions for improvement must be phrased in a kind and respectful way.

Explain all this to the students, to ensure they understand what's coming and will arrive prepared—both emotionally and materially with an extra printed copy—for next week's class.

Homework for Week 7: No reading assignment this week. Print out a fresh copy of the final draft Narrative Essay you turned in and bring it with you to next class.

Online Discussion for Week 7: You've now completed the first essay for this class. What was the hardest part for you? What was the easiest? Comment your answers below.

Week 8: Workshop Session 1; Return graded final drafts

THIS WEEK, THE ENTIRE class is devoted to a Workshop, following the instructions I noted in last week's lesson plan. I hold the graded final drafts until the end of class, so they won't be a distraction to the students.

*Optional Kindness for Warm-hearted Instructors: Because rewriting and improving an essay can only help students grow, and because I believe in second (third?) chances, I may offer one last rewrite opportunity to students: Any student who received below an A on the final draft and would like a chance to improve the grade may wait until after his/her essay is workshopped, and then use that feedback (plus my feedback on the final draft) to revise/edit/rewrite and resubmit the essay one last time. If they get a higher grade on this draft, it will replace their Final Draft grade for this essay. If I'm planning to do this, I let them know this *now*, so they will pay close attention to workshop feedback.

Here are the Workshop instructions once more:

- Each student will put a fresh copy of his or her final draft in the stack on the table.
- Each student will then come and take a copy of one essay (not his or her own) and sit down to read it. The student will not make notes or feedback, simply read. When finished, the student will return the copy to the table and grab a new one from the stack. I will allot 30 minutes of class for reading essays this way; however many the students can get through in that time.
- When the reading time is up, all essays go back to the table, and we form up into a circle for discussion. I will grab an essay from the table and read the title or summarize what it's about and then ask how many students read that essay. I will make a list on the board of how many read each essay, then we start discussion on the essay with the most readers, discuss it, and then move to the next essay on the list (this way, we're giving our best chance at a quality group discussion since hopefully a decent number of the students read that essay).
- Emphasize the importance of positivity in the feedback and the

requirement for the writer to remain silent (listening ears only) during the discussion, saving any questions for the end.

- The discussion itself is simple—I write two questions on the board: "What did the writer do *well*?" and "What could the writer improve?" We start with the "did well" list, then give a minute or two for quick notes on improvement at the end.
- The student who wrote the essay is not permitted to interject or explain during the discussion, only to take notes if desired. However, he or she may ask questions for clarification after the discussion of his/her essay has completed.
- Get through as many essays as you reasonably can in this way, and the rest will be saved for next week, when we'll repeat the process again.

Save just a couple minutes at the end of class for returning the graded final drafts of the essay. Then gather up the stack of undiscussed clean final drafts from the table, and set them aside to be workshopped next week.

Homework for Week 8: No reading assignment this week. Recover from having your essay workshopped (or prepare for having yours workshopped next week). On a piece of paper, write down the answers to the following questions (and bring it to class next week):

1. Did the Workshop process go as you expected? Why or why not?
2. What do you think writers can learn from having their essays workshopped?

Online Discussion Post for Week 8: If you had your essay workshopped this week, how did you feel about the experience? If your essay has not yet been workshopped, how did you feel about providing feedback on *another* student's essay during the workshop this week? Explain your answers in the comments below.

Week 9: Workshop Session 2

SO TECHNICALLY, THIS week is the start of quarter 2, but I built in this additional class period to allow time to finish up the Workshop if we were unable to get to all essays in the previous week. This week's class is devoted to finishing up the Workshop experience for the Narrative Essays. Repeat the Workshop instructions from the previous week, using only essays which were not already discussed. By the end of the thirty minutes of reading time, ideally all students will have read all the remaining essays, and everyone can participate in the discussions.

*Note: If you have a small class and finished up all the Workshop essays in the first session, you can use this week instead to break down what students learned from the Workshop process, using their homework questions as a starting point for discussion.

Be sure to remind students of the opportunity to revise and resubmit their final drafts, if you're affording them that chance, and to set a clear deadline—I usually give them one additional week (meaning any resubmitted final drafts must be turned in at next class).

*Additional note: If you have a large class and cannot get to all essays between these two sessions, either allow an additional class for workshopping if you have the room in the schedule, or as an alternative, have the few students who did not have their essays workshopped send you an electronic copy of their final drafts. You can then copy each of these into a Google Doc and recreate the Workshop environment electronically by having all students log in to the document and provide feedback on each essay where everyone (including the essay's writer) can see the feedback. Just be sure to set the Google Doc settings to allow *Comments Only*, so that students can comment but no one can edit or change the essay itself.

Homework for Week 9: Read "Chapter 6—The Basics" in Section II: Argumentative and Persuasive Essays as preparation for next week's class.

Revise final draft based on new feedback (if resubmitting) and bring a typed/printed copy to next class.

Online Discussion Post for Week 9: This week, answer whichever discussion question you *didn't* answer last week. So, if last week you commented on how it felt to have your essay workshopped, this week, comment on how it felt to provide comments on another student's essay. If last week you commented on how it felt to workshop someone else's essay, this week you should comment about how it felt to have your own essay workshopped. Post your answers in the comments below.

Week 10: Introducing the Argumentative Essay

GO OVER THE CONTENTS of "Chapter 6—The Basics" in class. Then hand out the Argumentative Essay Requirements sheet and Argumentative Essay Rubric (both are available in this book). Go over both documents aloud and answer any questions the students have. Be sure to emphasize the need for this essay to have a *three-prong thesis* and to clarify what that means, providing examples on the board. (If you aren't familiar with a three-prong thesis, be sure to read Chapter 7 prior to this class; it covers it in detail.) I like to do a class discussion where I throw out a simple, generic topic (like "Cats are better than dogs" or "Dogs are better than cats" and then have the class brainstorm supporting arguments, then choose the three strongest and write them out as prongs for the thesis as a demonstration). Also make sure to emphasize that this essay will require the use of research, citations, and a Works Cited page.

Homework for Week 10:

1. Read "Chapter 7—Planning and Outlining Your Argumentative or Persuasive Essay," then do basic research and choose a topic that fits within the prompt provided on the Argumentative Essay Requirements page.
2. Write a Thesis & Outline for your Argumentative Essay (using the information in Chapter 7 as a guide) and bring a typed copy of your Thesis & Outline to next class.

Online Discussion Post for Week 10: What are the elements of a strong argument in an essay? What can you plan into your thesis/outline to ensure that your essay will provide the strongest argument possible? Discuss below.

Week 11: One-on-One Meetings to Review Thesis/Outline; Group-Work Activity

THIS WEEK IS VERY SIMILAR to the Thesis/Outline week from last quarter. I meet individually with students to review and discuss each student's Thesis/Outline, and to help them restructure them if necessary so that all students leave class with what they need to write the first draft.

Before meeting with individuals, I divide the students into groups and give them a group assignment to do while they wait to be called. For this week, I like to do a review activity for *ethos/pathos/logos* to get students' minds on the right track for crafting strong arguments. One of my favorite such activities is a "Silly Argument" assignment, which goes basically as follows: I divide the class into two or three groups. On the board, I write three "silly arguments," such as "Squirrels are terrifying," "All girls should wear pink nail polish," and "Time travel exists." I assign one of these arguments to each group. Each group must decide together whether they are arguing *for* or *against* the statement, and then come up with at least three supporting points to make their argument—one that utilizes *pathos*, one that utilizes *ethos*, and one that utilizes *logos*. They should write these down and choose a spokesperson for their group. I allow them to fabricate sources, data, etc., as needed to serve as "supporting research."

When I finish meeting with students one-on-one, I have each group present their argument, stating which direction they're arguing, and providing their supporting reasons. The class then votes on whether each group's argument was convincing, based on the strength of their use of the rhetorical devices. This is a silly, fun assignment that students usually enjoy—but I make sure to remind them that for their own essays, they need to find *real* sources, not made-up ones.

Homework for Week 11: Read "Chapter 8–Selecting Credible Sources to Support Your Argument." Using the information in these two chapters, gather your sources for this essay (minimum 3 sources required). Write down all the info for these sources and bring to class next week.

Online Discussion Post for Week 11: Did you have trouble finding credible sources for this week's assignment? Did you come across any sources which were *not* credible? Discuss below.

Week 12: Discuss Works Cited pages; Review Research Principles

THIS WEEK'S CLASS IS devoted to a crash-course in citing sources. We'll be going into *much* more detail on this when we tackle Research Papers in quarter four; for now, the purpose is to get students acclimated to the concept that sources *need* to be cited, and to provide them a basic format through which to do so. For today, we'll use the Sample Works Cited Page and Sample In-Text Citations Page (both provided in this book) to show what a Works Cited page and in-text citations should look like. I print copies of these pages and hand them out to students so they can reference them as we discuss. As you over the examples, be sure to highlight how the in-text citation refers directly to an entry on the attached Works Cited page for that paper, and to point out details of the Works Cited page format, such as hanging indents, alphabetical entries, and carefully structured citations. Rather than going over details of how to format each citation entry based on the type of source, refer students to the OWL Purdue website (**http://owl.purdue.edu**[1]), which has a full handbook on how to format a variety of source types.

Also take time in class to review what students read in Chapter 8 about finding credible sources, and to answer any questions students may have about this or about the sources they've gathered so far.

Homework for Week 12: Read "Chapter 9—Tips for Writing Your Argumentative or Persuasive Essay," then write your First Draft of your Argumentative Essay, using the tips in Chapter 9 and your Argumentative Essay Requirements sheet to guide you.

Online Discussion Post for Week 12: What's the basic argument for your essay? Share in the comments here so you can all see what the others are writing about!

---

1. http://owl.purdue.edu/

Week 13: Peer Reviews; Collect First Drafts

THIS WEEK WILL BE VERY similar to Week 5 in quarter one. Students will be paired up for Peer Reviews, using the first drafts brought to class. Be sure to print and hand out copies of the Peer Review Questions (they're the same for every essay) to help guide students through the Peer Review process. Students should swap papers and Peer Review each other's work. When finished, each student should give the essay and Peer Review sheet (with written feedback) back to the original writer of the essay. The writer can read the Peer Review and ask questions and make notes for themselves as needed.

When students are all done with the Peer Reviews, I collect both the first draft essays (which may now have peer comments on them) *and* the Peer Review sheets. I'll be grading both—the Peer Reviewer gets credit for the review, and I add additional notes and feedback to both the Peer Review sheet (if I agree/disagree with the peer's feedback, I may note this for the essay writer) and to the First Draft essay (using marginal comments as I explain in the Parent/Teacher Guide section on writing feedback on essays). At next week's class, I'll be returning the Graded Essay/Rubric *and* the Peer Review to each student—not to the reviewer, but to the student whose essay was reviewed—so that the student has a plethora of feedback to use in revising the essay that week.

I also give students a heads-up that we're starting Workshop early this quarter—that we'll be workshopping the First Drafts, not the final drafts. They will need to print an additional copy of their First Draft this week and bring it to class next week for the Workshop and email an electronic copy of the same First Draft to the instructor. I know this seems like duplication, but there's a reason for it... it will all be clear next week.

Homework for Week 13:

1. Get a head start on revising your First Draft Argumentative Essay by implementing anything you already *know* needs correction based on your Peer Review experience. You will not have the Peer Review form in front of you (I'll still have it until next week), but do what you can

from memory.

2. Print an extra copy of your First Draft (whether you've revised it at all yet or not) and bring this to the next class and email an electronic copy of your first draft to your instructor (it's important to do both, for reasons you'll see next week!).

Online Discussion Post for Week 13: Were this week's Peer Reviews helpful? Why or why not? Discuss below.

Week 14: Return Graded First Drafts; Workshop Session 1

WE'LL BE DOING THE Workshop on the First Draft this quarter to allow students to experience the benefit of having additional feedback up front when revising their first drafts. I explain this, then hand back the graded essays & Peer Reviews, give students a couple minutes to look through them, and allow time to answer any questions students may have about my feedback.

Then, we launch straight into the Workshop, following the same model we used last quarter, but with a slight variation:

All students place their clean first drafts (the fresh copy, not the graded one) in the stack on the table. Each student grabs an essay to read (not his or her own). If the student finishes that essay before the time is up, they return it to the stack and grab another. Allow twenty minutes for students to read essays.

Then, circle up for Workshop time. Choose an essay more than one student read, and begin discussion, same as in the last Workshop. Allow 5-10 minutes for discussion, then move to another essay. However, here is the variation... Whichever essays did not get discussed in the live Workshop will go into a Google Doc for students to Workshop remotely during the week. Be sure to get these up into the Google Doc in a timely manner after class, set it to *Comments Only,* and invite all students to join the document so students can have access for this week's homework. (If you don't want to use Google Docs, you can probably figure out another way to do this, but Google Docs works great for these types of activities.) NOTE: You will need all students' email addresses for this, so gather those in class if you don't already have them.

Homework for Week 14: Access the online Google Doc for the virtual Workshop; all essays which were not addressed during the in-class Workshop should be included in this Doc. Leave comments on each essay in the Google Doc for that essay's writer, the same types of comments you would have said in class. Please leave *at least three* comments on each essay (though you can certainly leave more). Be sure to be kind and considerate in how you phrase corrections or suggestions for improvement!

Online Discussion Post for Week 14: Any questions or issues accessing the online Google Doc go here! If you accessed it with no trouble and already completed your Workshop feedback, drop an "I'm good!" in the comments below.

Week 15: Revision Week! Review Techniques/Tips for Revision

NOW THAT THE STUDENTS have their graded first drafts, Peer Reviews, *and* workshop feedback, they're ready to revise their Argumentative Essays! Use class time this week to go over the Revision Tips/Techniques in "Chapter 10—Revising & Editing Your Argumentative Essay," including reviewing the elements shown on the Argumentative Essay Rubric. You could even read parts of the chapter aloud in class if you want; it's a short chapter. Allow time for students to ask questions.

Homework for Week 15: Edit, revise, and rewrite your Argumentative Essay into a new draft, using the tips in Chapter 10 and the feedback from your graded first draft essay and Rubric, your Peer Review, and the Workshop.

Online Discussion for Week 15: What is your least favorite part of the editing and revision process? Why? Comment below!

*Note to instructor: If possible, try to reply to each "least favorite" comment from this week's discussion with an encouraging response.

Week 16: Collect Final Drafts; In-Class Activity

COLLECT FINAL DRAFTS of Argumentative Essays from students and set them aside to be graded.

Today's class will focus on a side-topic related to writing: cohesion. "Cohesion," in the sense I use it, is the idea that the entire piece of writing all fits together as one unit. In essays, this means that the essay remains focused on the main idea or thesis, and that appropriate transitions are employed to join ideas together.

I like to do a fun activity with the students to demonstrate what happens when cohesion does *not* exist in a piece of writing. This is especially fun with fiction, but it will work for essay writing as well. Here's how it works:

You (the instructor) take a sheet of lined notebook paper and write the first line of a hypothetical essay on it. Then pass the sheet of paper to a student (don't let any other students see what you wrote). That student writes the next line of the essay, doing his or her best job to continue the thought you opened with (but without any further help or clarification from you). They then fold the paper so that only their line is showing (yours is folded back) and pass the "essay" to the next student, who writes the next line, folds the paper so only the most recent line is visible, and passes it to another student. Continue on this way until there is one student left... this student should write the concluding line of the essay based on what it seen only in the line that's currently visible. (If you have a very small class, pass the paper around a few times to make sure you have almost a full page of lines before a student writes the "conclusion.") It's like a modified game of *Telephone*, essay-style.

Collect the paper and read the "essay" out loud to the class. It will probably be all over the place and ridiculous... and that's the point. This is what happens when thoughts are disjointed, and an essay doesn't have a clear, unified focus. Use this activity as a launching pad for a brief review on the importance of focus and a clear thesis in essays.

Homework for Week 16: In my class schedule, this is the last week before Winter Break, so I do not assign homework this week. However, if you would like to assign homework, you could always make copies of the in-class rambling essay and have them add transitions, etc., to improve its cohesion.

Online Discussion Post for Week 16: I do not assign a discussion post for this week (see explanation on Homework above).

Week 17: Return graded Final Drafts of Argumentative Essay; Introduce Quarter-3 Topic: Practical & Business Writing

RETURN GRADED FINAL drafts of the Argumentative Essay, with completed Rubric attached. Allow students a couple minutes to ask questions, then have them put the essays away.

Today we begin discussion on a very different type of writing: Practical & Business Writing. In class, go over the intro to Section III and "Chapter 11—Professionalism: Why It Matters" to set a context for this quarter's topics.

Open a discussion with students to brainstorm a list of different ways in which professional writing skills may be important for various career fields or life goals—I like to use students' actual goals for this, so see if any students are willing to share what their career or life goals are. If so, write these on the board and then guide the class through creating a list of potential uses for professional/business writing for each career/life goal. This helps students to better grasp the context for these skills, and why they're worth learning.

Homework for Week 17: Read "Chapter 12—Business Emails, Business Letters, and other Professional Correspondences" and be prepared to discuss in class next week.

Online Discussion Post for Week 17: Did you learn anything new from reading Chapter 12? If so, explain below. If not, describe what you think is the *most* important concept from Chapter 12, even if you already knew it before reading.

Week 18: Introduce the Business Email/Business Letter Assignment

THERE ARE NO FANCY Rubrics or requirement sheets for this; students will use Chapter 12 as a guide for writing their own sample business letters this week.

In class, take time to answer questions students may have about the Chapter 12 reading they did for homework. Then, open a class discussion to brainstorm scenarios in which a person may need to send a business-style letter or email in life. Allow students to suggest ideas and write them all on the board. These can serve as ideas for students to use in this week's homework.

Go over the two Example letters from Chapter 12 in the book, both the casual one and the businesslike one. Make a chart on the board comparing the two examples, and be sure to point out the defining aspects which set the business-style letter apart as more professional than the other.

Homework for Week 18: Think of a realistic scenario in which you might need to write a business letter, then write that letter (you may create a fictional recipient and scenario/reason for writing the letter if you need to, so long as it is a scenario which could occur in the real world). Use Chapter 12 as a guide to ensure your business letter is as professional as possible. Type up your business letter and bring it to next class.

Online Discussion for Week 18: Ask your parents if they have ever needed to write a business-style email or letter. If so, ask them for what situation/occasion they needed to do this. Comment your results below.

Week 19: Informal Peer Review of Business Letters; Collect Business Letters to Be Graded

HAVE STUDENTS TAKE out the business letters they wrote for homework, then pair students up and have them share their business letters with one another. Students should provide basic feedback on each other's letters via an informal one-to-one conversation—since there is no Peer Review sheet for this assignment, I like to just write two basic questions on the board for students to use to guide their discussions: What did the writer do well? What could be improved?

When all pairs are finished, take volunteers for any students who would like to share their business letters out loud with the class. If any volunteer, allow them time to do so.

Collect Business Letters, and explain to students you will be providing feedback and a basic grade for them at the next class, and then they will have a chance to revise and resubmit them the following week for a higher grade, if they choose.

*Note on grading this assignment: I did not create a Rubric for this assignment because the results can vary depending on what scenario/recipient the student chose. You can compare the letters to the basic concepts/examples from Chapter 12, and then provide feedback on what's done well, and anything that could use improvement. As for specific grades, this one is a little more subjective, but here's a general guide: If the business letter is well written with little to no need for improvement, it gets an A. If it's fairly well done but needs improvement in a couple places, it gets a B. If it meets most of the expectations but needs several corrections, it gets a C. If it lacks an overall voice of professionalism but still hits a small amount of the criteria for professionalism, it gets a D. If it does not feel professional at all and does not meet the majority of expectations for the business letter as outlined in Chapter 12, it gets an F. Be sure to provide feedback/explanation for any areas that need to be changed so the student will have direction when they revise.

Homework for Week 19: Read "Chapter 13—Resumes & Cover Letters," and be prepared to discuss at next class.

Online Discussion Post for Week 19: Do you find it difficult to write in a professional/business tone and style? Why or why not?

Week 20: Return graded Business Letters; Begin Discussion of Resumes and Cover Letters

RETURN THE STUDENTS' business letters at the start of class, and remind them they will have the chance to revise and resubmit them as part of this week's homework, if they desire. Allow a few minutes for questions, then have students put their business letters away.

Begin discussion of Resumes and Cover Letters. Because students have already read Chapter 13, you can open this discussion by asking what they learned from the chapter, or how much they already knew before going in. Use Chapter 13 as a guide to brainstorm a list on the board of the most important elements of crafting a strong Resume. Then repeat the process to make a list for Cover Letters. Allow time to answer questions.

Homework for Week 20:

1. Revise your Business Letter (if desired) and print out an updated copy to submit at next class as an opportunity to improve your grade.
2. Create a Resume for yourself! (Don't worry about the Cover Letter this week; we'll get to that later.) Be sure to use your *actual* information and experience to craft this resume, so that the resulting document will be of use to you in real life.

Online Discussion Post for Week 20: Did you run into any trouble creating your resume, or did you find it easy to do? Why? Explain below.

Week 21: Collect Revised Business Letters; Discuss & Collect Resumes; Review Cover Letters

AT THE START OF CLASS, collect any resubmitted Business Letters and set them aside to be graded this week.

Have students take out their Resumes, and open a discussion about their experiences creating them. What was difficult? How long did it take? Was any part of the process more complicated than they anticipated? Why did they choose the template/format they ended up using? Etc.

Have students pass Resumes up to you, and flip through them—if anything stands out to you which was done exceptionally well, comment on it to the class and explain why it worked (even if you keep the Resume anonymous). Set Resumes aside to be graded this week.

Do a brief discussion reviewing the important elements of a Cover Letter, as discussed last week and as shown in Chapter 13. Inform students they will write a sample cover letter for this week's homework.

*Note on grading the Resumes: There are countless templates students could use for Resumes. When grading the Resume assignment, focus not on an exact style or format, but on the overall professional impact of the Resume. Check that the student included all the necessary information; that all the job entries are worded clearly, concisely, and professionally; and that overall the Resume has a clean, professional feel. Provide feedback on any areas which need correction (and also those areas which were done well, of course!), and assign a grade using a similar system to the business letter: A= excellent; B = good; C = adequate; D = needs major improvement; F = did not fulfill assignment requirements.

Homework for Week 21: Review the Cover Letter segment of Chapter 13, then imagine you are applying for your dream job, and create a Cover Letter for your Resume. Use the correct contact info for your intended recipient, taking the time to figure out who the letter would need to go to, and to address that person by name in the greeting. Type your Cover Letter, print it, and bring it to next class.

Online Discussion Post for Week 21: To whom are you (hypothetically) sending your Cover Letter? Why did you choose this person?

Week 22: Returned Graded Resumes; Collect Cover Letters; Introduce "Chapter 14—Blogs, Online Articles, and other Public Writings"

RETURN GRADED RESUMES and allow a few minutes for students to ask questions about your feedback. Inform them they may edit/revise the Resumes this week and resubmit next week for a chance at a higher grade, if they desire.

Pair students up to do an informal Peer Review of their Cover Letters, using the same discussion prompts as before: What did the writer do well? What could be improved? Suggest that students take notes to be used for revision, if they desire, since you'll be collecting the cover letters to be graded. Collect Cover Letters and set aside to be graded this week. If students are unhappy with the grades they receive back next week, they'll have a chance to revise and resubmit the following week.

Open the discussion of Chapter 14—Blogs, Online Articles, and Other Public Writings. This is a brief chapter, and could easily be covered in class. Students will reread it at home this week for review. Use the discussion to emphasize the need for *awareness* in what students post online, whether they are doing so for business or personal use. What is posted online should be considered permanent, since it very well could become so. Emphasize discretion in online posting, and the potential for online forums such as blogs, online magazines, etc., to grow one's business or professional presence if handled thoughtfully and intentionally.

HOMEWORK FOR WEEK 22:

1. Review "Chapter 14—Blogs, Online Articles, and other Public Writings." It's a short chapter, so please read even if it was covered well in class this week. Then, it's time to do some research.
2. Locate a blog or online article you feel does professionalism *well* (i.e., it fits all or nearly all the criteria provided in Chapter 14). Print out a sample blog post/article from this site which exemplifies these

criteria, and bring it to next class.

3. Write your *own* sample blog post—but not online; just type it and print it. Your blog can be on any topic that interests you, and can take any tone—humorous, serious, informative, analytical—but it must meet all applicable criteria listed in Chapter 14 (include a basic description at the top of what your blog site would be called, what your overall topic for the blog would be, and what posting schedule you would follow; also give this specific post a title and make it clear how this post fits into your blog's overall theme). Print this sample blog post and bring it to next class.

4. Revise and reprint your Resume if you want to try for a higher grade; bring the updated copy to next class.

Online Discussion Post for Week 22: Do you follow any blogs or online article sites? If so, which are your favorites? Do they meet the criteria of Chapter 14? Why or why not? If *you* have a blog, does your blog fit the Chapter 14 criteria? Why or why not?

Week 23: Collect Resubmitted Resumes; Return Graded Cover Letters; Discuss Blog Examples; Review and Collect Student-Written Blog Posts

COLLECT RESUBMITTED Resumes from any students who chose to do so, and set aside to be graded this week.

Return graded Cover Letters and inform students they may revise and resubmit this week if they choose to do so.

Open class discussion about blog posts, and allow students each to share which existing blog they printed a sample from, and why they chose it. Have them read a short sample of the blog to demonstrate the blog's tone and subject matter. After each student shares, open a brief discussion about how that blog sample did or did not meet the Chapter 14 criteria, allowing the student who brought in the sample to take lead in the discussion.

Collect student blog first drafts; these will be graded and returned next week. Students should also print an extra copy of the blog post they wrote this week to bring for next week's Workshop.

Homework for Week 23:

1. Revise Cover Letters (if desired) and print an updated copy to submit next week.
2. Print an extra copy of the blog post you submitted this week and bring it for Workshop next class.
3. Read "Chapter 15—Social Media Etiquette" and answer the following questions on a piece of paper. Bring this to next class to be collected.
   a. Which principles appeared in both the Social Media Etiquette chapter and the Blog Post chapter?
   b. Did you learn anything about Social Media Etiquette you hadn't considered before? Explain.

Online Discussion Post for Week 23: Did you enjoy writing your own sample blog posts? Why or why not?

Week 24: Return graded Resume resubmissions; Collect any revised Cover Letters; Return Graded Blog Posts; Collect Homework Questions and do a brief discussion; Workshop for Blog Posts

RETURN ANY GRADED RESUME resubmissions and collect any revised Cover Letters from students who are resubmitting those this week.

Lead a brief discussion reviewing the main principles from "Chapter 15—Social Media Etiquette," then collect student homework questions to be graded. (I just give a completion grade for this.)

Return the graded blog posts and answer any student questions, then dive straight into the Workshop.

The Workshop will be simple this time... rather than dividing up the papers and having students read them before Workshopping, each student will stand up and read a blog post *out loud* to the entire class. It's up to you whether you have students read their own posts or have them trade and read each other's, but make sure all posts get read aloud, and while they're being read, note the title of each on the board so you can guide the Workshop after all have been read out loud. Then, pick one title at a time from the board and lead the class through discussing that blog post. Get through as many as you can in the remaining class time. Make this discussion fun and encouraging, centering the conversation on what each blog did well and whether/how it hits the major criteria from Chapter 14. The blog's author should remain silent during this process, but can ask questions for clarification at the end, as usual. If time runs out before all students' blogs are discussed, you can opt to follow up with a Google Docs Workshop session online this week, but because the week after this class is Spring Break for my students, I may not do this unless those students want the additional feedback.

Homework for Week 24: This is the week before Spring Break for my students, so I keep the homework for this week simple: *If* you would like to revise your blog post for a higher grade, do so this week. Be sure to print an updated copy to submit next class.

Online Discussion Post for Week 24: There is no discussion post for this week (see explanation in Homework above).

Week 25: Return any resubmitted Cover Letters and any other graded homework; Collect any revised Blog Posts to be re-graded; Introduce the final project for this course: the Research Paper

RETURN ANY GRADED COVER Letters which were resubmitted last week and any other graded homework papers, and collect any revised Blog Posts which are being resubmitted for a higher grade. Then jump straight into discussing the focus for quarter four—The Research Paper. Hand out copies of the Research Paper Requirements sheet and Research Paper Rubric (both available in this book). Go over these in class, allowing time to answer questions.

Homework for Week 25:

1. Read "Chapter 16—What Qualifies as a Research Paper?" and "Chapter 17—Deeper into Research." Both are short chapters.
2. Then, come up with a basic topic idea that fits the assignment requirements you were given in class. Do basic research to ensure there are enough sources to support your argument for this paper (you will need a minimum of ten sources!).
3. Write a basic Thesis & Outline for your Research Paper (you can use the brainstorming/outlining tips from the chapters on Narrative or Argumentative Essays to help you, if you need a review). Type up your Research Paper Thesis & Outline, print it, and bring it to next class.

Online Discussion Post for Week 26: How does a Research Paper differ from the Argumentative Essays we did in quarter two? How are they the same?

Week 26: Return any graded Blog Posts that were resubmitted; One-on-One Meetings to review & approve Thesis & Outline for each student; Group Activity while waiting

RETURN ANY GRADED BLOG Posts that were previously resubmitted.

Before beginning individual meetings to approve students' Theses & Outlines, assign a group activity that students can do while waiting to be called. A good activity for this week would be another ethos/pathos/logos review, since students will need to be fresh on these concepts for writing the Research Paper. One simple activity is to have students break into small groups, and then have each group take out a sheet of paper and divide it into 3 columns: *ethos, pathos,* and *logos.* Under each column, the group should brainstorm as many examples as they can of well-known commercials or advertisements (on TV, radio, etc.), which use that particular rhetorical device. For example, some lawyer ads on television focus entirely on the lawyer's credentials (*ethos)* rather than making an emotional appeal—if students can think of a specific legal company which runs ads of that type, that company could go in the *ethos* column.

Meet individually with students to approve each student's Thesis & Outline. Pay special attention to whether the topic is focused enough to make a strong argument, yet a popular enough topic where the student should be able to find adequate sources to support the argument. If any students need help revising their Theses or Outlines, take the time to help them do so.

When individual meetings are completed, have each group share the results of their group activities with the class.

Hand out copies of the Sample Annotated Bibliography (available in this book). This is a sample from the sixty-page Annotated Bibliography I had to create in grad school, which required two-page citations for each source. Point out that the students' annotations do not have to be this lengthy; they need only be four-five sentences each. However, be sure to emphasize the overall structure and format of the Annotated Bibliography, which students *will* need to emulate—alphabetical citations with hanging indents, and annotations continuing below each citation (also using hanging indents).

Homework for Week 26: This week you'll be going deep into the research portion of your Research Paper.

1. Read Chapters 18, 19, and 20, which cover Works Cited Pages, Bibliographies, and Annotated Bibliographies. These are all fairly short chapters.
2. Create an Annotated Bibliography for your Research Paper, using the requirements from your Research Paper Requirements sheet, the Sample Annotated Bibliography, and the information from Chapter 20 to guide you. You can reference the OWL.purdue website for information on formatting individual citations. Be sure to meet the requirements for number of sources, length and content of annotations, etc., as outlined in your Research Paper Requirements sheet. Type and print your Annotated Bibliography and bring to next class.

Online Discussion Post for Week 26: Do you have any questions about Annotated Bibliographies or Research Papers? Post them below, or if you have no questions, post "I've got this!"

Week 27: Collect Annotated Bibliographies to be graded; Review Argumentative Essay concepts to prepare for writing the Research Paper

ANSWER ANY QUESTIONS about the Annotated Bibliographies, then collect Annotated Bibliographies to be graded—make sure these are not the only copies students have, as they will need a copy to refer to as they write their first draft Research Papers this week.

Open up discussion about writing the Research Paper. Students will compose the first draft this week. The Research Paper Assignment is, at its core, a more complex Argumentative Essay, so this is a good time to pull out and review the Tips for Writing an Argumentative Essay from Chapter 9. Be sure to also review the Requirements sheet and Rubric to ensure all students are clear on what's expected from this paper.

*Note for grading Annotated Bibliographies this week: I use the criteria on the Requirements sheet as my parameters for grading this assignment. I provide feedback on what's done well and anything which needs correction or improvement, then assign a basic grade based on how well the Annotated Bibliography fulfilled the assignment expectations. (A = all expectations met with little to no corrections needed; B = most expectations met but a few minor corrections needed; C = meets most expectations but needs significant corrections; D = meets only some expectations and needs major improvement; F = does not meet expectations)

Homework for Week 27: Write the first draft of your Research Paper. Utilize your Research Paper Requirements sheet, Research Paper Rubric, and tips from Chapter 9 to guide you in the process. Type up and print out your first draft and bring it to next class.

Online Discussion Post for Week 27: How is your Research Paper going so far? Have you run into any problems? Is anything going exceptionally well? Explain below.

Week 28: Return graded Annotated Bibliographies; Peer Reviews; Collect First Drafts of Research Paper

RETURN GRADED ANNOTATED Bibliographies and give students time to ask questions if needed. There will not be an opportunity to correct and resubmit offered this week, because students will be asked to include a revised Annotated Bibliography with the Final Draft of the Research Paper in a couple weeks.

Pair students for Peer Reviews. Hand out copies of the structured Peer Review Questions sheet for students to write on for their Peer Reviews (available in this book). Allow students time to discuss the Peer Reviews with their partners and ask questions to clarify.

When Peer Reviews are completed, collect both the Peer Reviews and the First Drafts to be graded and returned next week.

*Note on grading these: as mentioned with the previous essay assignments, I give credit to the Peer Reviewers for the in-class assignment, then make notes onto the Peer Review sheet to expand on/clarify the Peer's feedback, in addition to providing my own feedback directly on the student's First Draft and Rubric.

Homework for Week 28: Get a head start on revising your Annotated Bibliography—it's not due until you submit your Final Draft, but you'll need most of your time next week to revise the paper itself, so it's a good idea to get the Annotated Bibliography ready to go this week.

Online Discussion for Week 28: Write some feedback on your experience with crafting an Annotated Bibliography: What did you find difficult? How much time did it take? Was it more difficult (or easier) than you expected? Explain below.

Week 29: Return Graded First Drafts with Rubrics & Peer Review sheets; Allow time in class for students to work on editing/revising or to meet one-on-one with you to ask questions.

THE ABOVE SUMMARY IS pretty self-explanatory. I'll add only that you can also ask the class if there are any Research Paper-related topics about which they would like additional instruction/clarification. If any students chime in, take a few minutes to cover the requested topics with the class.

Homework for Week 29: Revise your Research Paper using the feedback from instructor comments, Peer Review, and revision/editing tips from Chapters 5 & 10 of *Put Some Pants on That Kid*. Type up and print out your updated paper—and be sure to include your revised Annotated Bibliography! The Annotated Bibliography should be part of the same document as your Research Paper, so the last name & page# heading at the top right should continue sequentially through your Annotated Bib, picking up on the next numeric page number following the final page of your essay itself.

Online Discussion Post for Week 29: How's the editing/revision process going? Comment below with where you are the process and how the experience is going for you.

Week 30: Collect Final Drafts; Discuss Final Workshop Cycle

COLLECT FINAL DRAFTS of Research Paper and set aside to be graded. Open up a discussion about students' overall experiences with this Research Paper project—how they feel they did, what were the easiest/most difficult parts of the assignment, etc.

Inform students that we will use the last two weeks of class for our final Workshop sessions. Review how the Workshop process will work—it will be a bit different this time (see below)— and let students know that they must come prepared to *present* their Research Paper to the class next week. (Student should bring notes, a fresh copy of the paper, visuals, or whatever he/she needs to confidently present the paper to the class.)

The workshop for the following two weeks of class will take more of an oral presentation format. Students will be asked to get up one at a time to give a brief, spoken summary of their Research Paper. This oral presentation should include a statement of their thesis, a summary of the research they conducted to support their paper, and a basic summary of the arguments presented in their paper, culminating in a conclusion. After each student presents, there will be a brief Workshop session, where the class will discuss how they feel the student's argument performed in (1) use of *ethos/pathos/logos*, (2) persuasiveness, (3) clarity, focus, and organization, (4) use of supporting research, and (5) overall effectiveness. We will still focus on *what they did well* and *what they could improve*, but targeting these five categories for each presentation. We'll get through as many as we can next week and allow time for the rest on the final week of class.

Homework for Week 30: Prepare notes, visuals, etc., to present your Research Paper to the class next week during our Oral Presentations/Workshop Sessions. Think of this like a chance to distill your full argument (with basic supporting research) down into a speech of five minutes or less.

Online Discussion Post for Week 30: Post any questions you have about the Oral Presentation/Workshops here. If you don't have any questions, comment with "I'm good to go!"

Week 31: Return Graded Final Drafts; Oral Presentations/ Workshop Session 1

RETURN GRADED FINAL drafts to students.

Dive straight into the Oral Presentations/Workshop, using the instructions outlined in Week 30.

Homework for Week 31: If you did not present this week, make sure you're ready to present for next week's final Workshop session.

Online Discussion Post for Week 31: Next week is our final class! We'll be doing one final Workshop session... and then a party! We need everyone to chip in to bring something for the party, even if it's small or simple (like a bag of chips). Comment below with what food/drink you will bring for the party.

Week 32 (the final week!): Finish Oral Presentations/ Workshop Session 2; Party!

DIVE RIGHT INTO FINISHING up the Oral Presentations and Workshop session for any students who did not present last week.

When the Workshop is completed, it's time to party! I typically open up a generic discussion about how students felt about this class, what they found helpful, what they enjoyed or didn't enjoy, etc., for conversation while students enjoy the foods and drinks they brought for the party.

NO HOMEWORK OR DISCUSSION POST FOR WEEK 32—You're done!

Rubrics and Essay Requirements, Checklists, and Worksheets

NOTE: All Rubrics and Essay Requirement sheets are tailored to *my* preferences as a writing instructor. If you would prefer a different prompt, or need to modify the requirements for your own use, please feel free to do so.

Since this is an e-book, you will obviously not be able to write on worksheets or make copies from here. However, the link below will allow you to access downloadable/printable version of all the Rubrics, handouts, worksheets, and checklists mentioned in the lesson plans in this book:

Narrative Essay Assignment handout

Narrative Essay Rubric

Argumentative Essay Assignment handout

Argumentative Essay Rubric

Research Paper Assignment handout

Research Paper Rubric

Peer Review Questions worksheet

Self-Editing checklist

You are welcome to print and copy the materials included at the below link for both your personal use and for your students. I only ask that you not attempt to resell or otherwise repackage these materials, as they are intended as free resources which accompany the *Put Some Pants on That Kid* Student Book and Parent/Teacher Guide.

Printable versions of all the above documents are available on my website here:

https://www.ccrawfordwriting.com/pspotk-printables.

Other Resources

This section includes additional resources, such as sample Works Cited pages, sample in-text citations, and more. I understand these images may be small and hard to read, so I've also made full-sized, handout versions of them available to print on my website.

You can find them at the same resource link:

https://www.ccrawfordwriting.com/pspotk-printables.

Sample Works Cited Page

Crawford 18

Works Cited

Burton, Stacy. "Rereading Faulkner: Authority, Criticism, and *The Sound and the Fury*." Modern

Philology 98.4 (2001): 604-628. JSTOR. University of South Florida Library, Tampa, FL. 13 April 2008 <http://www.jstor.org/stable/439123>.

Faulkner, William. *The Sound and the Fury*. 1929. Ed. David Minter. 2nd Ed. New York: Norton, 1994.

Ford, Ford Madox. *The Good Soldier*. 1915. Ed. Thomas C. Moser. New York: Oxford UP Inc., 1990.

Levenson, Michael. "Character in *The Good Soldier*." Twentieth Century Literature 30.4 (1984): 373- 387. JSTOR. University of South Florida Library, Tampa, FL. 13 April 2008

<http://www.jstor.org/stable/ 441407>.

Sample In-Text Citation

Crawford 2

new focus. The novel centers on the Compson family, a family that has "fallen to pieces," and is "long in decline from its genteel Southern eminence, wrecked by scandal, drink, and madness" (Matz 28-29). Such a family would definitely not be considered respected or prominent in society, and yet, Faulkner chooses to focus on this family, even allowing the main portion of the narration to be carried by three brothers who take the reader "into psychic worlds of mental retardation, suicidal depression, and vengeful mania" (29). In choosing to have the story narrated through the eyes of the Compson brothers, Faulkner takes the reader into the mires of Compson family living, of gossip, dysfunctional relationships, and family disgraces. He provides the reader an inside view of life outside the spotlight of societal prestige and influence, and in doing so, brings a sense of true realism that is characteristic of the modern novel.

Crawford 4

Works Cited

Faulkner, William. The Sound and the Fury. Ed. David Minter. New York: Norton, 1994.

Kershner, R. B. The Twentieth-Century Novel: An Introduction. Boston: Bedford Books, 1997.

Matz, Jesse. The Modern Novel. Malden, Massachusetts: Blackwell Publishing, Ltd., 2004.

Note: These examples show the use of underlines for book titles; many formats now prefer the use of italics for book titles instead.

Sample Annotated Bibliography

*Note: the example on the following page is from one of my graduate school assignments and contains lengthy annotations (1-2 pages each); your Annotated Bibliography assignment will likely require far shorter Annotations (4-5 sentences, possibly more depending on instructor preference). However, this sample does illustrate the format of a typical Annotated Bibliography. Please note that the Annotations are formatted as part of the citation, continuing below it on a new line but with no additional spaces and following the indentation structure of the citation. Sources are also still alphabetized, just as they would be in a regular Works Cited or Bibliography. It is several pages long, so I'm providing only a few pages here in a rather small format, to save space but to still give an idea of visual formatting. You can find a printable copy of this sample Annotated Bibliography at if you would like to look at it in more detail.

Collaborative Writing: An Annotated Bibliography

Bonito, Joseph A, and Robert E Sanders. "Speakers' Footing in a Collaborative Writing Task: A
Resource for Addressing Disagreement While Avoiding Conflict." *Research on
Language and Social Interaction.* 35.4 (2002): 481-514. <u>LEA Online.</u> LEA Online.
University of South Florida Library, Tampa, FL. 5 Dec. 2007
<http://www.leaonline.com/doi/abs/10.1207/S15327973RLSI3504_4>.

This article relates a study that was done of a group engaged in a collaborative writing
task. The focus of the study was to examine the ways in which the members of the group
approached or dealt conflict. Bonito and Sanders found that the members of the group
adopted various "footings" in order to resolve conflict or avoid further disagreements.
They noted three "functions of adopting or changing footings" used during the course of
the group's collaborative activity. They state that the group they observed found a
middle ground between pursuing conflict and avoiding it, a way in which to moderate
conflict or to avoid the need for conflict altogether. In other words, they state that the
"participants have found a way of addressing and resolving agreements indirectly" (483).
Some changes in footing within the group appeared to be strategic, whereas others were
merely necessary for moving onward with the task. Bonito and Sanders state that there
are three main concerns with any collaborative task: content, wording, and inscribing the
text. As the members of the group discussed the content to be included in the project, if
they were discussing content which had already been decided upon, they were considered
to be in the footing of "author." If they were arguing for their personal preferences or
about specific wording, they were considered to be in the footing of "principal" (488). In

general, there are three types of footing exhibited: principal (when they express their own thoughts on content or what the text should say), author (when they speak about the wording of the text itself), and animator (when they begin to actually "inscribe" the text which they have planned) (489). These changes in footing allow the group to continue onward with the task, and to "avoid conflict while still addressing disagreements" (507). Bonito and Sanders claim that their study also provides important information for educators, as their findings "highlight features of collaboration that are consequential for acquiring writing competence" (507). They also point out that the identification of footings is complex, since the footings themselves are collaborative in that the particular type of footing is not identifiable until a response is seen in the footing or reaction of another member of the group. They argue that collaboration "compels participants to make public…their thinking regarding the topic and the writing process" (509). They also indicate that further research should be done on the topic of how (and if) these changes in footing impact the participants' learning process. This article would be useful for any instructor who uses collaborative writing in the classroom, as it provides insight into the complex dynamics of group interactions, and might allow instructors to more keenly perceive the subtle shifts in group dynamics, and to guide the students accordingly so as to make the process more productive.

Brockman, Elizabeth Black. "'English isn't a team sport, Mrs. Brockman': A response to Jeremy." English Journal 83.1 (Jan. 1994): 60. Academic Search Premier. EBSCO. University of South Florida Library, Tampa, FL. 5 December 2007. <http://search.ebscohost.com/login.aspx?direct=true&db=aph&AN=9405051951&site=ehost-live>.

This essay begins with an anecdote from the author's experience assigning a collaborative writing assignment to her class of high school students. While student reactions were mixed, one student, Jeremy, responded in a way that characterizes the sense of apprehension many students feel at the thought of co-writing an assignment: "English isn't a team sport, Mrs. Brockman" (60). In response to this, Brockman addresses her fellow high school English teachers and offers some tips for the implementation of collaborative activities in the classroom. The first tip she gives is to "begin with a good assignment." Brockman posits that there is no need to extend page lengths or otherwise inflate assignment requirements so as to make it collaborative – nearly any assignment can be turned into a collaborative one. The next piece of advice Brockman gives is to "select writing teams with care." Brockman forms teams of two to five students, and takes into consideration student requests for group partners along with student ability levels. In this way, the students are paired with classmates with whom they are likely to work well. The third tip Brockman gives is to "conduct writing workshops." Brockman argues that class time should be given to allow students to discuss, draft, comment, and revise their joint document. She also suggests that computer labs are convenient because of the accessibility for students to write and make immediate changes; however, collaborative writing workshops are highly time-demanding due to the fact that students must be allowed time for discussion before beginning the writing itself. The fourth and final suggestion Brockman provides is to "allow for variation in writing processes." This is important, as there is no "right" way to write collaboratively, and since each group member may have a different writing process, the groups will need time and the freedom to be flexible and to readjust the roles of the group members as needed.

This article offers four simple but helpful recommendations for any instructors who wish to implement collaborative writing in the classroom. Due to the concise nature of this article, it would make a convenient reference or reminder for teachers even once the collaboration process has been implemented. The suggestions that Brockman offers are both logical and practical, and would be valuable advice for any collaborative writing instructor.

Bruffee, Kenneth A. <u>Collaborative Learning Higher Education, Interdependence, and the Authority of Knowledge</u>. 2nd ed. Baltimore, MD: Johns Hopkins University Press, 1999. 4 Dec. 2007 <http://www.netlibrary.com/summary.asp?id=63780>.

This book addresses Bruffee's beliefs that universities should be viewed "not as stores of information but as institutions of reacculturation", and that professors are "not purveyors of information" but "agents of cultural change who foster reacculturation by marshaling independence among student peers" (xii). Bruffee argues that collaborative learning actually helps students to learn more effectively and to productively construct knowledge based off of interactions with their peers, the same as they will do through interactions in society once they leave the university. Bruffee points out that collaboration is common in the workplace and in life; common, in fact, everywhere but in educational settings. This is why he emphasizes the importance of collaboration among students and also between instructors and students within the classroom (xiii). Collaborative learning, according to Bruffee, views knowledge as socially constructed, and therefore values the idea of social interactions being used to further learning. Part I of this book, "Collaborative Learning and What It's About," discusses Bruffee's discovery, as a newly appointed department head for Freshman Composition, that he and others in his field were at a loss as to how to teach writing to incoming students. Bruffee and the others, after much discussion, realized that their students came into the classroom not as blank slates, but already accultured to speak and write in ways determined by the society from which they came. In other words, what was deemed "unacceptable" in the writing classroom had been acceptable in the students' respective communities, and therefore, the students were feeling isolated from the classroom community and unable to repair the breach between the classroom community and their own. As such, Bruffee and the others determined that writing classrooms must be largely responsible for the "reacculturation" of the students – to teach the students the language and techniques necessary to become an "acceptable" part of the writing classroom and the academic community (7). This reacculturation is accomplished, in large part, by collaboration among students and teachers alike, in the formation of a "transition group" which allows students to "renegotiate [their] ties to one or more of the communities [they] belong to, and at the same time gain membership in another community" (8). Part I of the book then goes on to discuss several methods of using collaboration within the writing classroom, including Chapter Two on consensus groups, Chapter Three on teaching writing as a "collaborative, conversational process" (55), Chapter Four on changing classroom social structures to create a collaborative environment in which knowledge can be shared and formed, Chapter Six on peer tutoring, and Chapter Seven on the use of computers to facilitate collaboration. Chapter Five of Part I provides a brief history of the development of collaborative and cooperative learning. Part II of the book addresses some major topics regarding the ideology of education and the assumptions of authority and knowledge.

Acknowledgments

I would like to thank my team of early readers for their valuable feedback and input on the *Put Some Pants on That Kid Materials*:

Thank you to M.J., Christy, and Beth, for taking time out of your summer to read a writing textbook! Your feedback, as always, was greatly appreciated.

Thank you to Michele Wilson for reading my early version of these materials, and for providing valuable insight into how better to package them so that they could be of maximum use to their intended audience. I am very grateful for your feedback!

Contact Me

If you enjoyed this book, **please take a moment to leave a review on the book retailer where you purchased it.** These reviews are a *huge* help to indie authors like me... they help persuade new readers to give my books a try!

Want to see more from me, outside my published books? Come find me where I hang out online!

If you love **clean young adult fiction** and want a portal where you can read a bunch of my clean YA content, interact with me and other readers, and help me build a community around clean YA fiction, **check out my Story Subscribers portal on my website!** Find out more on the next page, or at **http://ccrawfordwriting.com/storysubscriberscontent**.

If you'd like to receive updates on future releases, behind-the-scenes info on my writing, and personal updates, subscribe to my monthly email newsletter at **http://ccrawfordwriting.com/subscribe**. I never spam my email subscribers—you can expect one email per month, with occasional bonus emails if I have a new release, sale, or something important to share. And you'll even get free story downloads for subscribing!

I'm also on social media! You can find me at:

Website: **http://ccrawfordwriting.com**[1]

Blog: **http://ccrawfordwriting.com/blog**

Facebook: **http://facebook.com/ccrawfordwriting**

Instagram: **http://instagram.com/ccrawfordwriting**

YouTube: **http://youtube.com/ccrawfordwriting**

---

1. http://ccrawfordwriting.com/

Or contact me directly through email at **ccrawford@ccrawfordwriting.com**. I'd love to see your comments and respond to any questions you might have.

Thank you so much for reading!

Also by Crystal Crawford

Legends of Arameth
The Edge of Nothing
The Path to Paradox
The Ends of Exile
The Lex Chronicles Trilogy E-book Collection

Put Some Pants on That Kid Essay Writing Curriculum
Put Some Pants on That Kid: A Writing Handbook for High School and Beyond (Student Book)
Put Some Pants on That Kid: A Writing Handbook for High School and Beyond (Parent-Teacher Guide)

Secret Messages Sweet YA Romance Series
I'm Not a Stalker
The Five Suspects

The Leyward Stones
Macchiatos, Faerie Princes, and Other Things That Happen at Midnight
LeyGuards, Faespells, and Other Things That Breach the Veil
Fae Curses, Dark Kings, and Other Things That Must Fall

About the Author

Crystal Crawford writes clean YA fantasy and clean YA romance (and a smattering of other genres) in Florida, where every natural body of water hides something that could eat you, and if they don't get you, the weather might. She lives with her husband, five kids, two cats, one doofusy dog, and two live-in grandparents, who have all supported her dream of writing and drinking far too much coffee. Her imagination is her happy place! (But a deserted beach is nice, too.) When she isn't writing, she enjoys reading, napping, watching shows with her family, working in the garden, and homeschooling the kids, though most days you'll also find her doing laundry.

Read more at ccrawfordwriting.com.